Random Thoughts Revisited

Ronald W. Vasicek

Bloomington, IN  Milton Keynes, UK

authorHOUSE™

AuthorHouse™
1663 Liberty Drive, Suite 200
Bloomington, IN 47403
www.authorhouse.com
Phone: 1-800-839-8640

AuthorHouse™ UK Ltd.
500 Avebury Boulevard
Central Milton Keynes, MK9 2BE
www.authorhouse.co.uk
Phone: 08001974150

First published by AuthorHouse 4/27/2006

ISBN: 1-4259-2901-X (sc)
ISBN: 1-4259-2902-8 (dj)

Printed in the United States of America
Bloomington, Indiana

This book is printed on acid-free paper.

Dedicated to my children,

Andrew and Erin,

who gave me the time of my life.

Contents

Introduction   ix

Children   1

Attitude   23

Teaching   27

Religion   35

Forgiveness   41

Love   45

Thinking   51

Truth   55

Personal Responsibility   59

Giving   69

Material Wants   73

Nature and Conservation   77

Comfort Zones   81

Sports   85

Mr. Spock   89

Life's Balances   93

Differences   97

Goals   101

Authority   105

Exercise   109

Behavior   113

Epilogue   117

Introduction

These are the wanderings of an uncomplicated mind in search of truth.

There is no intent in these pages to dazzle you with statistics, no endless pro and con discussions, just thoughts gathered from reflective moments in one person's life. Most of what is written on these pages has probably passed though your consciousness at one time or another. The truth is not hidden from us if we but look. Some call it common sense. You might also think of it as using that funny round object on top of your shoulders.

This is the second edition. As time passed new thoughts crossed my mind at the strangest times; driving to the store, in a doctor's office, just as I am about to doze off to sleep. Ideas scribbled on bits of paper and napkins thrown in a basket which needed to be written. And besides, my son's picture graced the cover of my first book and I needed to give my daughter some press. So she is on the cover of this second edition.

Children

Children must not enter your life as a biological accident. Two persons' sperm and egg getting together to form an embryo is relatively meaningless compared to the act of parenting the resultant child. Any pair of fools can have a baby. Get a male and female together at the right time and voila, a baby. Birds and lizards do it. Whoever raises a child is the real parent not the biological couple. This should be stressed in school and be the guideline used by our courts in assigning custody.

If a parent gives away a child at birth, the true parents of that child are those who raised her. It is inappropriate for either the child or biological parent to search for the other. We place too much importance on biology, not near enough on child rearing. To those who gave away their child, "That child is no longer yours, forget her." To the given away child, "Love the parents who raise you and forget about where your egg and sperm came from. They are not important."

Why do people have this irrational pride of having made a baby? In fact shame is often more appropriate; a 17 year old unwed parent; people with 5 children who cannot properly clothe, feed or care for those they already have; or someone who after 5 years has produced a spoiled obnoxious brat. No pride is justified till you have raised a child who is an asset to our society. Perhaps this irrational pride stems from the fact, having babies is something they can do and "sadly" feel proud of without having done anything for which they should be proud.

Your baby means just that. The baby is yours. Someone else should not have to care for your baby. You should not have a baby till you have the time, money and emotional stability to care for the child yourself. You should not have to rely on your parents.

You must not need your children. One measure of a successful parent is when they produce adults who at 18 or 21 walk out the door capable and independent, not needing their parents. Their future depends on not needing their parents. Love the parent but do not need them. As I wrote this book, I realized many things I have written about have their roots in people's tendency to not think much of themselves. They try to derive their worth from their children, marital partner or favorite athletic team rather than from within themselves. Remember, you are the cake in your life; other people are just the frosting. Your legacy in this life is you. Your children are but one small part of you.

No one should have a baby for self serving reasons; a baby might save our marriage, fulfill my unattained goals, give me something to live for, make me feel good about myself. Before children are born is the time to evaluate who you are, determine your faults and work to correct them before children are born. Being a successful parent requires already having your own house in order. If not, the child will suffer from your inadequacies.

Marriage is not for the adults. They can survive without any commitment. Marriage is for the children. Children thrive in a stable environment with a male and female set of parents. The children make it important for us to intelligently pick the right mate and have the strength to make the marriage work.

The original intent of marriage was to provide a stable environment in which to possibly raise children. The likelihood of raising an emotionally, physically healthy child is greatly increased by nurturing from a stable male and female pair. Our society is improved by the production of a greater quantity of emotionally, physically healthy adults. Therefore marriage of a male and a female is a very desirable arrangement.

Things have gotten out of control. Marriages do not last and marriage has come to revolve too much around financial benefits rather than raising healthy children. Society gains no value from giving financial advantage to people who desire each other's exclusive companionship without ever having children (i.e. without becoming a family). There is nothing wrong with desiring another person's exclusive companionship, but there is no reason for us to pay people to do this. We need to pass legislation defining two types of unions. The simplest such union, let's call it a Companionship, would be a union of two people who wish to formalize their desire for each others exclusive companionship. There would be no economic value to this union. There is no family so taxes, health care, etc. would continue to be each person's individual responsibility. Only when a child is born or adopted would this change.

Once a child is introduced into a Companionship consisting of one female and one male, financial benefits could result if the couple commits to a more permanent union we will call Marriage. Marriage would be defined as the union of a male and female who have dependent children. The Companionship union could be easily dissolved but a Marriage would be very difficult to end. The greater difficulty could consist of a mandatory waiting period with counseling to resolve differences and whatever other efforts are found to be effective in maintaining marriages. It is in society's interest to help parents raise healthy children so we must help them financially and encourage them to preserve the Marriage. If one person chose to remain home and care for the children the couple would be eligible for additional benefits, such as our current married couple tax rates. Something similar would be available if one person in the Marriage died. If both continued to work, they would continue to file individual returns. However, in either case, the couple would be eligible for dependent deductions (probably bigger than currently) for their children. They could take this deduction for up to 3 or 4 children. The purpose of the deduction is to help parents raise a reasonable number of healthy children not to encourage over population which is endangering all of us.

Obviously this is very different from our current laws and we would need to iron out many details. So much has changed in our world. We no longer need to encourage people to have children, we are overpopulating our world. We no longer subjugate women and relegate them to the home.

This brings us to the awesome responsibility we take on when we decide to have sexual intercourse with someone of the opposite sex, in or outside of marriage. If you do not want a child you must be extremely careful in your prevention. Even with the most careful prevention a child is always a possible outcome. You must be ready to assume the responsibilities of parenthood if a child results. That means the person you are having sex with must also be committed to this possibility. You must not enter into a sexual relationship lightly. A human being's future may rest in your hands. Sex carries an immense load of responsibility which our shortsighted selfishness encourages us to forget.

Children are a vocation not a part time job. The most important endeavor many of us will undertake in our lifetime. One of the few impacts most of us can have on mankind's future. Let's suppose every child born from this day forward were raised without irrational fears and hatreds and taught to treat everyone else as they would like to be treated. The world would be a paradise in one generation. Not a material, but a behavioral paradise. You say "Impossible" and maybe that is true. Perhaps an attainable goal for all parents would be to raise children who are a little better than themselves. A few generations would produce significant improvements in our world. You've heard the saying "People will rise to meet high expectations." Have parents forgotten this? Where are the high expectations for their children's behavior? Parents have many excuses why they are not met. A couple of the worst are; "Children are like that" and "I was like that when I was a child." Two to the biggest cop outs used to avoid the hard task of improving the values and behavior of our society. Acceptance of these two statements is bending to the same peer pressure which can mold our children to inappropriate life patterns. Perpetuated because not enough of us have the strength to go against what society passes off as normal. The whole point of raising children is to produce offspring better than ourselves, making the world a better place. As a parent you have the wonderful opportunity to shape your child's and the world's future.

On a personal note, it took me ten years to decide I wanted children. My decision was a result of the realization; this was my greatest opportunity to have a positive influence on a very troubled world. Adults were extremely difficult to change but children could be guided in the right directions with great care. I knew if I had children they would become the most important thing in my life for the next several years. Nothing could be more important. I could never trade them in like a used car or get a new one like a job. I had to get it right with them. I also knew if I did it right, my life would be richer. I read all the parenting books and took from each what was not rubbish. And there is a lot of rubbish about being your child's friend and negotiating. Forget it, you are in charge. It is hard work, just do it.

Indeed my parenting years have been the best years of my life. I have enjoyed nothing more than being my children's father, sharing their lives as they have grown. They were joyful, happy, untroubled and fun to be with virtually always. I never felt I needed a break, someone to take them off my hands for a day or two. Indeed by today's standards, my parenting experience was so good it was surreal. I like to think it is because we practiced what is written on these pages. I hope this gives all my readers hope because raising children need not be painful. It can be an absolutely wonderful experience. I have learned and been changed more by this experience than from any other aspect of my life. How can one engage in bad habits, selfish, unkind, uncouth behavior if you hope to instill the opposite in your children?

We frequently hear that children do not want mom and dad around. They want to be with their friends. This is true to some extent, just as it is true the parents want to spend some time alone with their adult friends. However I encourage all parents to enjoy their children by being involved in their lives. Coach or assist their sports teams, at least attend the games, be their scout leader, a chaperone at school functions, have family outings, go out of your way to be with them. The time when you can be so close to them is short. I believe if you are truly involved in their life, they will enjoy having you around and your parenting experience will be much more enjoyable. For this to succeed you must enjoy children. But then you should not have had children if you do not enjoy them!

I said nothing could be more important than your children. This does not mean you do not have a life. Everything in life should be done in moderation. Your life needs to be balanced. Do what is reasonable for your children and expect some help from them. Children will not be around forever. You need to develop your own life. You also decrease the possibility of selfish, self-centered children if your activities and needs occasionally preclude the child's. Children learn there are people other than themselves that matter. They learn their parents are people too and they matter. All your parenting will be a balancing act. Give children a lot of time, attention and love but expect kindness, attention and consideration in return. Never overindulge them with material things. This is one area that is almost impossible to err on the too little side.

There is a lot more to life than having babies. Hopefully you will have a full life before and after them or if you have none at all. Seems like as we grow older, all we look forward to is having grandchildren. I would like to think we have goals in life that do not revolve around children. In the Stone Age we needed them to prevent extinction. Having children is no longer a necessity. Raising good ones is.

And, by the way, grandparents should not spoil their grandchildren. They should treat them precisely as they would have treated their own. Being a parent is hard enough without your parents screwing up your children by spoiling them.

It is a shame how little we help people be better parents. We must pass a test to drive a car or fly an airplane because we might hurt someone if our skills are inadequate. There is no requirement to have children! Children are the future of our world! If we mess them up we hurt them, most likely others and the world in general. Parenting classes should be a required subject in high school. Not simply how to change diapers. High school students should be taught the immense difficulty, responsibility, commitment required and the importance of having your self straightened out before having children. No one should be allowed to graduate without demonstrating a complete understanding of the skills required of parents.

You have heard people say, "That is not suitable for children to watch, hear, do...." Did you ever wonder what the world would be like if adults thought of those same things as not suitable for themselves? Our society leads children to believe smoking, swearing, drinking excessively and indiscriminate sex are privileges and signs of mature adults. In fact they are signs of immaturity in adults. The inappropriate ways adults deal with the problems and disappointments which occur in all our lives. Instead of becoming strong within themselves they look for ways to hide from their problems. Hiding is easier in the short term but a recipe for failure in the long term.

It's the oddest thing. Everyone says example is the best teacher and yet we violate this principle constantly in our own homes and then wonder "Why is my child like this?" We use indecent language, cheat on our income tax, speed on the highways, cut in line.... It is difficult to point to anything parents tell their children not to do or to do which is not also good advice for the parent. If we conducted our adult lives as we desire of our children, the world would be a wonderful place.

I think we warp our children at a very early age. We talk about boyfriends and girlfriends at an age when they should look on the opposite sex as merely another friend. Why must we tease our 5 year old about their girlfriend in kindergarten class? Why put makeup and earrings on a 4 year old? Is it because sex is such a pervasive influence on all we do? We are not allowing our children to be children. I think it best to delay as long as possible the time when a boy looks upon girl as a sex object rather than simply as their friend.

Big boy/big girl. I hear this directed at our 2,3,4,5 year olds. Somehow it seems wrong to me. Like, there is something wrong with being little. My god they are only around 3foot tall. This is another subliminal message from adults, "We want you to be like an adult as fast as you can". We convince them youth is an undesirable stage in life rather than a stage to be savored just as every other stage. Seems silly but I think truth lies here. Much better if we said, "Wow look what you can do. That's great." This Big Boy image pushes them to want to consume alcohol, nicotine, etc. because, of course, this is what big people do. Savor youth, do not shortcut it.

And yet on the other side we turn our children into dependent babies. We do their homework and science projects. We drive them to the bus stop or worse to school. When they have trouble with a coach, teacher or other student, we talk to the coach, teacher or parent rather than let them work it out. And when finally they have babies of their own we become grandparents who feel we must relieve their children of their parental duties.

But when your children signed up for children they signed up for a 24/7 job. And, by the way, why do we teach our children to say Mommy and Daddy rather than Mother and Father?

There is always the discussion over what is inherited and what is not. I believe our most important attributes are learned. We inherit intelligence, physical attributes, maybe even our strength of will. However, we learn our values and attitude. These are what enable us to live a peaceful, loving, gentle life; the real determining factors in the quality of our lives. Seems people want to believe we are mostly a product of genetics and little can be done to change a person. This relieves us of guilt or the necessity of working hard as a parent to shape the future of our children. Especially when this means we need to improve ourselves to provide the necessary good example to shape our children's values and attitude. What a message you would send if your child saw you give $10 back to the cashier when she gave you too much change, you slow down to let someone on the entrance ramp merge into expressway traffic, you are ill and still are pleasant to others.

Genes are unchangeable. How this genetic makeup unfolds in our life is greatly impacted by our parents and our own determination. Genetic traits can be enhanced, redirected or minimized by subsequent teaching. A person could be a great athlete genetically but if directed elsewhere by their parents they may never be an athlete. A person could be genetically antagonistic. He could become an obnoxious adult but with proper direction he could become a leader in our society by directing his antagonistic tendencies toward attaining difficult goals.

A good attitude is one of the greatest gifts we can give our children. However we cannot give it if we do not have it.

Children are like clay. One strong whack seldom produces the desired result. Repeated consistent massaging will, but it must be done before the clay hardens.

Raising children is not significantly different from how any person should interact with any other person.

Have fun with them

Enforce your rules and hold them accountable

Practice what you preach

Be kind, respect and appreciate them

Expect and demand kindness, respect and appreciation in return.

Children can be taught anything. It is more difficult to teach the right than the wrong things. Children's struggle for identity, independence and meaning in their life make selfishness and rebellion an easy outcome. Even easier, if parents accept this as an unavoidable part of growing up. There will always be some of this, but with the proper expectations all our families and our world could be more like "The Nelson's". Parents have always had the power to transform our planet into a world of peace in one generation but not enough of them have had the strength and understanding to exercise this power correctly.

Children learn by example but good example must be accompanied by discipline. Administered at an early age it is very effective. The longer you wait the less effective it becomes. Discipline is one of the kindest things you can do for your children. Properly administered it is an act of love not power. Consistent consequence, not punishment is the most helpful aid in reinforcing this teaching. The ultimate goal of discipline is the establishment of a strong conscience (values and attitude). If doing the right thing is to be instinctive, discipline must come from within the person not from external sources. A person's conscience, not punishment imposed on them by others, must become the reason they do the right thing. Having a conscience means you care about how your actions affect others. This can be as direct as cutting in front of someone in line or as indirect as throwing trash out your car window. Laws and punishment are vital tools for maintaining order, given the current low state of our society's conscience. However our goal must be to decrease dependency on these tools. Laws and punishment do not produce a long term improvement in societal behavior. This will only happen if a strong conscience is produced in our children, making laws obsolete.

Discipline can be difficult. Remember the only power children have over parents is to make them give in by wearing them down. Giving in seems like the easy way out, but it is like a lie. The lie never solves the problem it only requires more lies to hide the original lie. Telling the truth solves all the problems but it is the thing people find so hard to do. Same with discipline; giving in seems easier. This relieves the immediate aggravation but the aggravation will be there again tomorrow and the next day and the next.... Taking a definite stand (hard as it seems) eventually gets your point across and eliminates the reoccurring problem. Oddly, many people do not do the obvious right thing. The moral: Most good things require short term pain in the beginning to insure long term success. This manner of enforcing authority is not unique to a parent child relationship. It applies the same in adult to adult. Anyone in a position of authority maintains respect for their authority by consistently applying the rules and consequences for violation of the rules. It is a very simple concept. The penalty for not doing this is chaos whether it is within a family, workplace or country. We do our children and ourselves a great disservice by expecting less of them than we should.

There is a correlation between liking oneself, feeling secure and a person's ability to be considerate, kind and sharing. A child who feels secure is probably the one who shares his toys. The one screaming and complaining, "He took my truck" is probably the one who does not like himself much and feels insecure. These children grow into insecure adults who do not completely like themselves. These are the adults who zoom around all the stopped traffic and cut in at the last second and do the same thing in any line when they can get away with it. The ones who walk in front of the car in the supermarket parking lot rather than taking the tiny detour behind, so the car need not wait for them. And when they are walking in front of the waiting car, they walk like a snail.

There are many subtle ways we influence our children to be secure and sharing. Did you ever share an ice cream cone or an order of fries with your child? Or take the toast you slightly over toasted for yourself rather than give it to a family member. Don't you think this sends a powerful message to your child?

The most important lesson children must learn is for them to like themselves and know they are the most important person in the world to themselves. This frees them from being threatened by others or from feeling bad because of what others do to them. Oddly, being secure within your self allows you to treat your needs as secondary to others. In most cases it really does not matter if you are second. It is kind of a hard concept but intensely liking ourselves allows us to be more considerate of others because we do not feel threatened. Only when we are legitimately threatened do we come first.

We place too much emphasis on children working. We say it instills responsibility. Maybe it does but it also seems to instill an undesirable emphasis on the material part of our world (The need to buy "Things"). Some work is fine but parents are the ones primarily responsible for instilling responsibility in their child. What moral values, attitude and work ethic they learn from you will be much more important than what might come from a part time job. They will be working for 40 years after school. Teach them responsibility but let them use these school years to discover the world outside the money arena. It is very likely they would grow more as a decent human being by participation in Boy or Girl Scouts, band, religious groups, school clubs, or community volunteer activities than from most part time jobs.

We do our children a great injustice trying to foist off on them the idea everything is equal in life. If we gave Johnny a 10 speed bike for his 10th birthday, we must do the same for Amy. If we spent $100 on Amy for Christmas, we must for Johnny. This encourages the feeling of entitlement so rampant in our society. The fact is people get different things for a host of reasons. Sometimes it is as simple as, some people deserve more than others at particular moments in their lives.

This old fashion idea keeps popping into my head. We would all be better people if we were required to earn what we want in life. This applies to all aspects of life from our job to our family. We must teach our children, doing the right thing earns huge rewards. If one child has proved to be more trustworthy, they should be rewarded by giving them more freedom than a less trustworthy child. Perhaps the trustworthy one might be rewarded by being allowed to stay out till 10 rather than 9. If one has been more pleasant, helpful, worked harder at school; this behavior should be rewarded with special privileges; maybe extra use of the car or a party with friends. Isn't this how we encourage better behavior? And yet it seems people think we should not treat one child different from another.

So often I hear people say they like being with their grandchildren because they get to be kids again with them. Why can't we always be kids? I find it sad as we grow older; we lose many of the good and retain many of the bad aspects of children. The selfishness and thoughtlessness we keep. We lose our imagination, innocence and ability to enjoy simple things. Society convinces us we cannot be happy unless we indulge ourselves with all the man made pleasures which quickly become repetitive and boring, requiring us to buy the next gimmick to keep our interest. We lose the kid in us and become boring adults when our children are gone. We should do the same "kid" things before we have children, during the parent years and after our children are gone. We should be putting up Halloween, Christmas and Easter decorations, swinging on the swings, riding the merry-go-round, jumping in the leaves, watching Snow White, our whole life. What happens to us?

Two of the most abused words are No and Don't. These words should only be used when you really mean it, only to enforce a rule which is truly important. How many times have you heard a parent say "Don't Run"? Now, get serious, what child does not run? What a silly thing to say. Yes they might fall and hurt themselves. Most likely they will suffer no great damage from the possible fall and any damage they do suffer will be a learning experience for them. If they never fall they will never learn. We learn a great deal from our mistakes. Hopefully we learn from the relatively harmless mistakes. Besides you are not going to make them stop running. Let children make the relatively harmless mistakes and perhaps they will grow up a bit wiser. By constantly saying "Don't" and not enforcing the "Don't" you reduce the value of your "Don't." Just as bad, if the parent actually enforces the "Don't" in these silly instances and creates a very sheltered child. Or how about "Don't go out without wearing a coat". They always go out anyway. What harm is done? They will discover they are cold by themselves. They will not die and they might just learn something. Again this "Don't" is simply not appropriate. Reserve the "Don't" for important things like, "Don't cross the road unless I am with you", to your 3 year old. Now this is important. You are not preventing a possible bump on the head you are preventing the possibility of their being dead. You cannot learn anything once you are dead!

There is another very dangerous word we teach our children, "Mine". It is the seed of selfishness. Most things in a family should be "Ours". You should share as much as possible. An ice cream cone, soda at the movie, Bigify it at McDonalds and share the fries. Little things like this form a sharing attitude.

Here is a list of thoughts I gave my children; various ideas which struck me as I passed through life.

To: Andrew and Erin,

* I love you very much
* The greatest gifts you will ever receive come from the heart not the wallet. Never judge a person's affection for you by what material gifts they give you.
* And conversely, the greatest gift you can give is your love.
* Each person is unique but we all share many human frailties. Most of your friends have or will experience the same problems as you. Many people put up a big front to hide their problems, but hiding never solved any problem.
* Save some money from every paycheck. Regular savings over many years will grow surprisingly large.
* Color, creed or social position should never be used as a measure of a person's worth.
* Being kind and gentle does not mean you have to be soft with no backbone. Sometimes true kindness is tough as nails.
* Treat each person in your life as you would like to be treated.
* Think about other people. If you are walking across the street at an intersection and you see a car waiting for you to clear the intersection before they can turn, move a little faster.
* Eat fruit.

* There is no law saying we must get flabby and fat as we grow older. Life will be better if you take care of your body.
* Take advantage of free exercise. Avoid elevators, use stairs.
* Don't waste time in parking lots looking for the closest spot. You will actually save time pulling into the first spot which will not require backing out when you leave.
* Misery is infectious, but so is happiness. If you feel bad try to make someone else feel good, it will probably make you feel better also. If you make them feel bad how will they be able to help you feel better?
* There are many more good than bad people in the world. There are some very dangerous people. Be careful, but do not let fear of evil inhibit your life.
* Be happy with yourself, but always strive to be better.
* Never allow another person's unhappiness make you unhappy or another person's anger make you an angry person.
* Others (parents, siblings, friends, spouses) are important in your life. They add to the richness of life. But others will come and go, the only constant is you. Ultimately the richness of your life depends on you. Enjoy yourself.
* Each day you awake be glad you were blessed with another day to enjoy and help others enjoy. The world is difficult at times, but filled with wonder and joy if you just reach out for it.
* Happiness will not come from big things. Big things do not happen very frequently. A rich life comes from enjoyment of the day to day little things; a beautiful sunset, a flight of geese passing overhead, a rainbow, a smile.
* Nature is marvelous. Enjoy it often.
* Rise early. Morning time is so peaceful. You cannot see nature's beauty at night.

* Our world is very noisy. I think because people are afraid to stop and think. Have frequent quiet times by yourself. It promotes peace and thought.
* When you get older never forget what it was like when you were younger. The excitement of youth is often lost along the way and we often forget we did the same "silly" things when we were younger.
* Humility is a virtue we could all practice more.
* You will make mistakes. Learn from them.
* There is no job with more potential to transform the world than parenting. Using their experience to help the next generation become better. What a paradise the world would be in a few generations if we could do this. A parent's big cop out is saying "I did the same thing when I was their age. What else should I expect?"
* The only person you have to impress is yourself. Don't be something you don't want to be just to gain someone's friendship. You don't have to be a fake for a real friend. Choose friends wisely.
* When choosing someone as a friend or someone to admire and seek advice from, look beneath their skin and rhetoric. People wear these like a clown wears makeup.
* Happiness is a state of mind that comes from inside you. No person or thing can make you unhappy unless you allow it.
* When life gives you lemons make lemonade.
* If it is partly cloudy, it is also partly sunny!
* The satisfaction derived from material things is fleeting at best.
* Never envy others. There will always be someone with more than you. Some deserve it and some do not. What others have is beyond your power to control. If you want something do your best to attain it and be happy with the results.

* Use medicine sparingly. Every minor headache, etc. should not call for an immediate aspirin. Your body's natural defenses will work better if you let them train. And if you learn to deal with the minor aches and pains you will find it easier to deal with the major ones that medication can only reduce to the minor level.
* Keep your (and encourage others to keep their) waste and trash to a minimum. Each of us thinks our wasted cup of water or bit of trash is insignificant, but multiplied by millions of people it becomes huge.
* Say what you mean. Don't make people guess. They often guess wrong.
* Never lie.
* Sometimes you must say what you mean and tell the truth in a gentle way.
* Avoid a rigid, structured life. Joy lingers in spontaneity.
* TV has some merits in small doses. Much of it is a danger to impressionable minds, or just a plain waste of valuable time.
* Know yourself. Be realistic.
* Never compromise your principles. Once you do something you know is wrong, it becomes much easier to do it again and again.
* It is difficult to speak the truth when people do not want to hear it. But if no one has the courage to speak the truth, the truth is never learned.
* Honor your commitments.
* Be on time. A 9 0'clock appointment does not mean 9:01; plan on 8:50 or8:55.
* Practice moderation in all things.
* Remember the irritating things others do to you. Don't be guilty of the same behavior yourself.

* You are responsible for your own safety. All of us will do stupid, unexpected things. Whatever you are doing always, "Look both ways."
* Read about everything. Ignorance breeds many of the world's problems, social and economic.
* If you truly understand another person it often becomes difficult to harbor hate for them.
* Get proper rest.
* Eat a good breakfast.
* Trust is a precious gift. It is difficult to build and it can be destroyed by one thoughtless act.
* Close doors behind you, turn lights off when you leave a room, put things back where they belong, close lids on containers,.... Seem like little things, but they set an attitude in your life of doing the right thing.
* Never wish to be older or younger. Savor the unique experiences at each age.
* There is no more powerful teaching/leading tool than your example.
* The ultimate goal of rules (laws) is not punishment. It is guidance. We should obey rules not from fear of punishment, but because we know it is the right thing to do.
* If you think a rule is wrong, work constructively to resolve this.
* Never worry about what "might" happen.
* Many of life's problems are self inflicted; poor spending or saving habits, poor health habits, not being a proper parent, having a bad attitude.
* Avoid putting off till tomorrow what you could do today. Most things we put off until tomorrow never happen.
* If you borrow something, return it without the 'borrowed from person' having to ask for it back.

* And lastly, I will always love you. One of my greatest joys in life has been being your father. I never dreamed raising a child could be so much fun. You are both wonderful people who will enrich the world.

Love,
Dad

One final word on children. There is a low level of mental illness which cannot be repaired by parents. Aside from this, most of the remainder of the world's problems are due to parenting which for some reason did not reach its highest potential. We pass on our bad behavior, irrational fears, prejudice, envy, insecurity, and bad attitude. Parents create our world's future. If you take nothing else from this book, take that one simple fact.

Attitude

Your attitude is the greatest factor contributing to the quality of your life. Incredibly, this most important thing in your life is totally in your control. You and only you choose to have a positive or a negative attitude. We cannot change what people do or say. We cannot change the past. We cannot change the level of our mental or physical gifts. We cannot change the inevitable. But we are in control of our attitude; how we react to what life has in store for us. And this choice overwhelms every other aspect of our life.

I saw a survey which found some newly wed couples found bliss and other couples fought. They wondered why. I do not think this is rocket science. Isn't the reason, some people learned how to get along in kindergarten and some did not. Everyone has problems. Some have a good attitude, others do not. Those with a good attitude know they are not the center of the universe and most things are not worth fighting about.

> Years fly by
> Like clouds changing shapes
> Ever different
> Not better or worse
> But the same substance
> Combined anew
> The wind controls the shape
> But we control the meaning

Teaching

Successful parenting depends on our example and discipline. If you live a kind, caring, disciplined life and you expect the same from your children, there is a high probability your children will fulfill this expectation. We hear "Our schools are not doing their job. Look at the kind of child coming out of high school." But the problem rests in our homes not in our schools. Schools teach knowledge, homes teach human values. Schools should teach human values also, but it is difficult for schools to change behavior patterns and attitudes instilled in the first 4-5 years of a child's life by their parents and constantly reinforced in their home during the next 13 school years. Make no mistake. If an unhappy, unkind, uncaring, poorly adjusted child is delivered to our school system in kindergarten, the chances are very high of the same type of person exiting 13 years later.

Some trumpet the need for huge increases in spending to improve student performance. But the quality of student performance is much deeper than the money to buy computers, modern gadgets and higher paid teachers. If our families do not provide children who want to learn, there will be little improvement from increased spending. The amount of effort and spending required to correct parental inadequacy is incredible. Up to date equipment and teaching techniques are simply icing on the cake. They will enhance the learning experience, but are not the biggest factors in student performance. An eager mind in the simplest learning environment will learn incredibly more than the unmotivated mind in a technologically marvelous environment. And oddly enough, good parenting is absolutely free. It is something all of us should be doing in our day to day lives as parents.

We should not use the term "low performing school district". Place the problem where it belongs. Low performing families are the problem. We hide the problem by saying the school is performing lower than desired. If a dam develops a hole, does it make any sense to build another dam further downstream? The hole in the original dam should be repaired. Unfortunately, it is a lot easier for us to throw money at schools than attack the problem in our own homes. The impact of school on a child's character is small compared to that from the home. Some people believe peer pressure will overcome family teaching. I believe a truly strong character/attitude instilled by the parents will usually prevent damage from peer pressure. Any school can teach most any child if the child wants to learn. Our schools should be as great as we can make them, but it is very difficult for schools to correct the problems instilled by our families. The desire to learn comes from our home. Getting this right corrects all the downstream problems; poor school performance, crime, angry/unhappy people. Why don't we concentrate on the one problem causing all our other problems, rather than on the hundreds created by this one problem?

The most important learning provided by our schools is not facts or principles but the love of learning, especially in the early years. Natural selection points to this, with the more touchy/feely teacher gravitation to elementary school and the more fact oriented teachers to high school. The most important learning for the majority of us occurs in elementary school. We learn (or at least there is the attempt to teach) all the social skills, how to get along with others, follow the rules and those in authority. We learn the basics of reading, writing, addition, subtraction, division and multiplication. And most important we learn to learn. The basics everyone needs to survive. We learn a lot of great stuff later; more complex math concepts, reading, science, history, etc. But for most of us if we got it right in elementary school everything else is just icing on the cake.

History courses should not just teach dates and names but rather the reasons events occurred. How we can improve the probability of good events and decrease the probability of bad events in the future by learning the causal relationships from history. You know the old saying "Learn from our past." Do you see any evidence we do this? We have been making the same mistakes since the beginning of time. There is a huge unfulfilled potential in history; if we could learn from the mistakes made by others and figure out how to teach this.

There is a trend today of not wanting to differentiate between students. (Actually this trend of promoting mediocrity is throughout our society, not just in the classroom.) Such as eliminating student class ranking or no valedictorian. Our country has been made great by people working very hard to be as good or better than someone else. What is wrong with recognizing the highest performers? This gives all the rest of us a goal. Reality is, everyone is not equal. There is a small percentage at the top, a small percentage at the bottom and the majority somewhere in-between. The argument is, we do not want to make the lower performers feel bad. Rather than worrying about people feeling bad when others do better, we need to teach reality. Which is; everyone needs to work as hard as they can to be their best and have the strength of character to accept that there will almost always be someone who will do better. We need to teach our children to accept and be happy with themselves as long as they are doing the best they can. They should be happy there is someone at the top end of the bell curve. That person at the top may be the one who invents the cancer cure that saves their life sometime in the future.

Most of us are not earth shakers, but we are each important. We perform some needed function and help the world keep moving along. Only a select few are earth shakers. People like Einstein, Michelangelo, Galileo, who bring forth new ideas, concepts or inventions that change the world forever. Allowing mankind to evolve to a better state; mentally, spiritually, physically. Without such people throughout history we would still be shivering in caves, wondering where our next meal was coming from. We need to provide the environment to encourage the growth of the earth shakers.

Teaching or parenting is not a bed of roses but there is potential for moments of enormous satisfaction. The opportunity to influence the quality of mankind is enormous; to influence a few young people in a kinder, gentler more inquisitive direction. I hope all teachers remember what you felt like when you were 6. Remember the tiny things which filled you with joy and wonder and also fear and anxiety. Remember how small events had profound effects on you life, good or bad. Remember what you wanted then and now is for others to treat you with respect and dignity. Children are people too. Remember your childhood and you will be a better teacher or parent. Children look for direction from us, but we generally fail as a society to give them the right direction. Instead of kindness and gentleness we give them envy and hate. You as a teacher or parent have some influence to correct this. We all can, to a lesser extent, in our day to day contact with others. We are all teachers in a small way by the way we live our lives.

Change the world? Most likely you won't. But that is not the issue. Doing what you know to be right is the issue. No one person has a significant impact on mankind's behavior patterns. Even great figures like Jesus have little impact on humanity's direction in their lifetime, if ever. Jesus was murdered as were many of his followers and can we honestly say the world is significantly different due to his time here? There are religions in his name, but was man's behavior significantly changed? Maybe a bit, it's hard to tell. The important thing is everyone can have a small effect on humanity's direction. Nothing will ever change if no one takes the first step.

Don't believe those who say do this and that good thing and you will change the world, everyone will thank you and everything will be wonderful. It won't happen. Do believe that if you do what you know is the right thing you will feel very good about yourself and the world will still be crazy and people will try to take advantage of you and a lot of bad things can still happen to you. However you will have an inner peace that can carry you through anything and because of your good deeds more people will be willing to help you in your times of need. You will not have changed the world but you will have had a small positive impact which is better than none or a negative one. We are in this world such a short time, it seems we would want to have had at least made a small positive contribution. Maybe that is the strength of religion. I think all of us would like to have accomplished something more worthwhile and lasting than the small pleasures we experienced in our brief stay.

Religion

Whether god does or does not exist should have no impact on your behavior. There is no logical reason to do anything but strive to be a good person. The better you are the better the world will be and the likelihood of your happiness increases. The role of religion should be to help us be better people. The form of your god or manner of worship is not important as long as the central message is goodness. This message is what is important not the method of conveyance.

There are so many religions with so many origins. Somehow the trappings of religion get in the way, distorting the central message of most religions. The prophet who supposedly brought the message or the particular form of your god becomes more important than accomplishment of good works.

Seems to me the core of most religions is the desire for each of us to be gentler, kinder, more compassionate, and for us to treat all others as we would like them to treat us. We should seek this goodness not to gain salvation or avoid punishment, but because it is the right thing, the only sensible life to lead because it makes life more enjoyable. If your brief stay here on earth was happy and you made the world a happier place, your time here was well spent. If there is a reward beyond life for being a good person, then so much the better.

In my mind a god is not a god, if belief in him requires believers to hurt people simply because they believe in a different god. If such a god were in fact real, he would not be worth following. He should be destroyed (or we should die trying). It boggles the mind how much suffering has come from people trying to impress their perception of god and religion on other people. Let religion teach the basic rules we all know are needed to help mankind live in peace with one another. Let god reside within each person as they perceive god. We all know what constitutes a good person but none of us may ever know the true nature of god.

I always thought it odd that everyone fighting in a war thinks god is on their side and he wants them to kill the other guy. Somehow I think killing people was never part of god's plan.

Some people would say "If you do not believe in my god you are doomed to eternal damnation." My answer is "You are making god in your own image; a mean spirited, jealous, vindictive god. If that truly is god, then I want no part of his afterlife anyway. It sounds no better than what we now have here on earth." I believe god would simply expect us to be a good person. Goodness is not something complicated. If you are happy and you are making the world a happier place you are doing the right thing.

I hope there is something after our physical life on earth. If there is not, I want to be sure I made a positive contribution toward leaving a better world for those who follow me. We get too hung up about god and not enough about what is really important, being a better person.

> Would the sky be less blue
> If there were no one there to view
> The heavenly scent of a rose less pleasant
> If no one was present
> Should you lead a good life
> Out of fear of some omnipotent god
> Or merely For Goodness Sake

Doing the right thing is hard. In the short term the wrong thing seems easier and more fun. But doing the right thing is like an insurance policy. It increases the chances of good things happening and decreases the chances of bad things. Problem is, many people lose sight of the long term. They often get away with the wrong things for a long time before it catches up with them. The person trying to do the right thing has to suffer through being mocked as a "Goody Two Shoe." But if you stand by your beliefs, each individual can make a difference, each person must make a difference. We have the power to break the world's endless cycle of selfishness and cruelty. But it is not easy. It means we often must be different and oppose what the world condones and what we find convenient for ourselves. If you do make a difference you will be happier by virtue of making the world a better place.

Religion has always been at war with science. Which has often been strange since the persecuted scientist was often extremely religious. A perfect example was Galileo. He had an intense belief in God, but had proof the earth revolved about the sun rather than the Catholic Church's belief in the opposite. The church banned Galileo's writings and put him under house arrest. The war has not been raged by the religious scientist, but by the religious dogmatic zealot. The difference between the two sides being, the religious scientist believes God created an incredibly beautiful and complex universe and gave humans a brain to enjoy figuring it out. The dogmatic zealot believes God told us what we need to know. We need not think. We only need to trust and believe. The religious scientist believes we are constantly learning and refining our understanding of the universe. They are engaged in the incredibly joyous struggle to understand. The religious dogmatic zealot prefers to have life be more like a cookbook that never changes. Again I come to the one central idea. The purpose of religion should be to lead us to become better human beings. It matters not what god, prophet, or set of beliefs which bring us to that state. It matters not why we are a good person, only that we are.

Forgiveness

Forgiveness is good, but can be abused if there are no consequences for the forgiven mistakes. Some treat forgiveness as a right not the gift which it is. The word "Give" resides in the center of the word. Ever find yourself tired of hearing the words "I am sorry?" Forgiveness is a noble thing, but if over used it is destructive. Forgiveness is earned by not having to be forgiven very often and by paying the consequences of the mistake being forgiven. Something is broken if forgiveness becomes habitually needed. Repeated mistakes indicate that the magnitude of the consequences paid by the habitual abuser probably needed to be increased! Seems like the prevailing attitude is; saying your sorry makes everything better. Well I am sorry too, but it does not. It would be much better if you had not made the mistake which required the "I am sorry." Depending on the nature and magnitude of the mistake, the "I am sorry" may be enough; especially if this is the first mistake. However, the "I am sorry" might only reduce the magnitude of the consequences they must pay for repeated mistake. It is amazing how mistake free people become when they know they will pay for their mistake!

Love

Life would be meaningless without others loving us and us loving them and ourselves. Our initial response should always be to offer love to a person. However that person must earn the love which is offered or it is forfeit. The world would be a better place if we did not treat love as an entitlement but rather as something to be earned. This is true for friends, family and spouses. Love is not much different from a job. Everyone has an equal opportunity but once hired they must perform. A few failures are not justification for firing, but lack of trying and repeated failures are. Something earned is more valuable to us than something given. Unearned/given things tend to spoil and rot. It does not matter if the given thing is money, job or love.

Many of us search for a very close relationship with one person and many of us marry that person. We say we love that person, but what does this really mean? What is this deeper love many of us seek?

What isn't it?

Not a starry eyed attraction.

Not sex.

Not about changing someone. Better like them as they are. Change is unlikely.

Not a magical gift of what you do not already have (happiness, confidence, self-respect). If these are not inside you no one can give them to you.

Not easy

Not a "Soul Mate". The idea there is only one person in the world perfect for each of us is a rather odd idea. There are approximately 6 billion people on this planet, of which you meet (on a close basis and at the right time) perhaps a few thousand. Out of this tiny sample you will pick one to love deeply. There are 6 million more groups of 1000 you never meet. So there are at least 6 million others out there just as perfect for you.

What is it?

It is a friendship closer than any other in your life, which you are committed to work hard to maintain and make grow.

It is a chance to change the world by raising children who will make the world a better place.

Love is a growing, living thing. It starts as a tiny seed when you meet someone you like because they were nice to you and fun to be around. If you take care of this seed, it begins to sprout and grow. Each time this person does something nice for you and you for them the sprout of love grows. Each time you share a fun event you grow closer and your friendship grows stronger. Your friendship grows by showing you care for that person by doing things as simple as picking up something they dropped, holding a door and letting them go through first, letting them have the last popsicle or sharing yours with them. If your trust, respect and sharing are strong enough the tiny seed grows into the beautiful flower we call love.

We tend to "fall" in love too easily with too much emotion and not enough thought. As I said, love is a growing thing, not a starry eyed attraction. Many people are deeply hurt when a professed undying love dies. This has happened to most of us. It would seem if this happened to you and you remembered the pain, the pain would encourage you to not do this to someone else. But learning from our past does not seem a strong point for us humans. As with any gift, our love should not be given easily. Be absolutely sure of what you are doing before you profess your love for another. It is very painful to take it back. If children are involved, it can be disastrous to them.

Love is wonderful, but we must remember love is not magic. Perhaps you heard the love song words "Everything I am is because of you." Love helps us, but who we are must come from inside ourselves. Our strength to weather life's storms must come from inside ourselves. The only constant in your life is you. Family and friends move away, become alienated, have troubles of their own, and everyone dies. But if you are strong by yourself you will always be there for yourself and you will have extra strength to help others. Don't look for some magical person to solve your problems and make your life worthwhile, look inside yourself. Liking yourself is the most important thing you can accomplish in your life.

Take time to meet someone you like as a person. A person you enjoy being with. And if parenthood is your vocation, someone you feel can help you raise children who will benefit the world. A person you want as your best friend

Thinking

Wouldn't the world be happier and better if we were more aware of those around us and how our actions affect them?

You're on a sidewalk crossing a driveway. Watch for cars wanting to turn into the driveway and step up your pace to allow them to turn sooner. Adjust your speed to allow someone to merge on the expressway. Stop and move that garbage can which has blown into the road and everyone is weaving around. Smile at people you do not know passing in the mall or standing in the checkout line. There would be much less anger in the world if we were more aware and cared more about people we encounter in life but never know.

I thought the purpose of a turn signal was to warn other drivers of your intended upcoming action. "I am preparing to start changing lanes. There seems to be plenty of space for me to do this." Why are so many already in the act of turning when the signal comes on? Using the signal then is useless; everyone can see you are turning. These people seem to be saying, "I am changing lanes now. Get out of my way."

When the movie ends, do not get up and stand there in front of those sitting behind you. Move quickly out of the way.

It seems to me so many people simply do not think. The evidence is everywhere. Many people do not vote. Many never read anything having any instructional value. People do not understand how their wasteful actions multiplied by billions of others doing the same thing have a huge impact on our environment. How little people think can be seen by the effectiveness of advertising; getting people to buy stuff based on nothing but emotion, looks or unsubstantiated fancy words.

Here is a little test which helps define how much a person thinks. Someone uses the toilet paper and there ends up being perhaps not enough for the next person. Do they; A) Notice this and replace the old roll with a new one, leaving the old roll on top for the next person to finish or B) Just place a new roll by the old roll for the next person to change or C) Do nothing or D) The worst case being they use all the paper and leave the roll empty?

Super size is great if people would think. Super size one meal for $.50 extra and get one other sandwich. Share the large fries and drink and save money.

The instant people step into their house or car on goes the TV, radio, or stereo. What is wrong with simply listening to the music of the birds, frogs, crickets, wind, or falling rain? What is wrong with quiet? To me constructive thought and noise do not go together. I have come up with plans of attack for many problems during long quiet rides, or at least I have gained some peace to allow me to deal with the problem.

All the conveniences we have today can make us soft, complacent, intolerant, non-adaptable and unthinking. Calculators, computers, air conditioners, automated cash registers, and endless rules/regulations reduce the need to think on even the simplest level of how much change to return to the customer. This does not seem like a big deal, but I believe in the past life has provided more stimuli to keep people from becoming stagnant and unlearning.

There is so much knowledge available today. We know so much about the universe around us. But many of us have chosen to understand so little. I have met people who do not know our sun is a star. Not that most people cannot have a basic understanding of science, they choose not to be interested. I cannot help but think everyone would be so much more excited about their life if they had a basic understanding of the wonders being discovered.

Truth

Truth is often much bigger than ourselves, our tiny circle of existence.

Truth is often not popular. Peer pressure makes it very difficult to speak and live the truth. Of course people do not like to hear the truth when it deals with a failure or weakness of their own. Personally I think the kindest thing you can do for a friend is show them reality. Frequently unhappiness stems from not seeing ourselves as the rest of the world does. If I see myself exactly for who I am, I know with what I am dealing. If I have some failing or weakness, I can decide what to do about it; live with it, realizing the rest of the world is aware and this might have a negative effect on my acceptance in the world, or I can try to improve myself. People say they want a more truthful world. However, when push comes to shove they cannot deal with it. I do not think they understand how simple life becomes when you always tell the truth.

There is no more worthy pursuit in life than the search for truth. Lack of understanding is regrettable. A lie is an abomination. If we all had our feet firmly planted in reality (truth) our world would be a magnificent place.

Difficulty facing truth leads to atrocities such as the Nazi treatment of the Jewish people in WWII, what we have done (are doing) to our environment, and many traumas in our daily lives. Some people believe "white" lies are OK. They help lubricate a relationship. Baloney, lies are always bad.

Never lie. Even seemingly harmless lies are bad.

For example, if your husband or wife asks, "Do you like my hair", and you do not, it is important to tell the truth. The forcefulness of the truth you must tell depends on how great is your dislike and the importance of the issue. All lies are additive and encourage more lies to hide the first lie. They place a barrier, a discomfort between people. Knowing people's true feelings gives us a choice; change, compromise, or ignore the feeling. An unknown problem cannot be resolved and often grows bigger the longer it takes to surface. How many times have you read a book, or watched a movie when a main character hides a truth? Could be the love they feel for someone which they hide for fear of rejection. Could be a dark secret they are afraid will damage the possible relationship which we all know is more easily forgiven early in a relationship rather than later. Don't you want to yell, "Say it!" to them? Do not let this happen in your life. Or if they do not love you back, wouldn't it be better to know right away so you will not waste any more of your time pursuing them. You can move on with your life. Or if your friend makes fun of you because of some belief or fear or yours, they are probably not worth having as a friend. You need to find a new friend.

And for Pete's sake do not lie to yourself. If you deny your value you will not take full advantage of the assets you possess. If you deny your failings you will not be able to correct them and improve. In either case you allow your life to be less than it might be otherwise. It is not always failings we deny but often just reality. We dislike admitting we are overweight, not the greatest athlete, not as smart as Jane. We must admit who we are, work to change what we do not want to live with, and acknowledge what we choose not to change.

Personal
Responsibility

We, through our government, have been encouraging feelings of entitlement and a lack of responsibility for our actions and choices.

Every citizen should be required to perform 1-2 years of service to our country; could be military service; could be helping the disabled by providing transportation, meals or companionship; could be teaching a trade to someone on welfare. Citizens would assume the roles (rightfully ours) which we have been pushing onto others in the form of our government. By pushing off these responsibilities we are losing one on one contact with each other, losing understanding and feeling for those less fortunate than ourselves, losing a sense of gratitude for all we have. Oddly we do not see (by asking the government to do our work) our taxes must increase dramatically and we must work longer to pay these taxes. I think if we spent more time one on one helping our fellow man we would actually end up with more time and we would feel better about ourselves.

A professional military is vaguely unsettling to me. So frequently professional armed forces are used by influential people to overthrow elected governments throughout the world. Seems unlikely in our country, but I would feel more comfortable with military composed mostly of 2 year draftees with a small core of career military, as it was in the past.

We must help others. But we must help them intelligently. We destroy people and families by giving to them and expecting nothing in return. Some people will always need and deserve our help due to medical problems, etc. However most people should be helped to make themselves self sufficient, an asset to society, and more importantly increase their self esteem. Often the hardest and greatest love is to not give, but instead help someone earn what they want. Plus there is the negative offshoot of government taking more and more of the roll of charity away from the private sector (people helping each other on a personal basis). We become less concerned over others. We become more selfish. We become unaccustomed to helping our neighbors. We do not even know our neighbors.

We give tax breaks to those who choose to have larger families. Maybe this made sense back when increased population was desired, but we do not need more people now. Having a baby is a free choice. If people want more children they should shoulder the responsibility.

Health insurance premiums should be per person. The current system of charging the same premium for families with 1 or 10 children makes no sense. Why should those who exercised responsible family planning and lived within their means finance those who chose to have 10 children!

Frugality is discouraged. Frugal people are not thought of in endearing terms but rather as cheapskates or tightwads. People talk about being frugal but they do not have the discipline to do it and they seem to resent those who do.

We punish people for responsibly planning for their future by saving. If a family saves for their child's education, doing without luxuries, they are penalized by being eligible for less financial aid vs. a similar family which chooses to be irresponsible, buys fancy cars, boats, clothes and saves nothing. Or the child eligible for $10000 in government aid attending a $20000 per year college. If the child works hard to win scholarships worth $10000, they take away the $10000 in government aid and he still ends up paying $10000, same as if he had exerted no extra effort.

The negative response to privatized social security is yet another example of our refusal to expect personal responsibility and lowering the bar on what we expect from our citizens. Those opposed say some people will not invest wisely and will be worse off than under our current government operated plan. For starters, almost anything our government does is inefficient so I find it hard to believe most of our individual citizens could not do better. Probably a small minority will make non-ideal decisions. However should we penalize the vast majority who would be much better off under a private system because a very few will not be quite as well off? Remember, it is unlikely anyone would go broke they would just have a little less. There is no question after 30-40 years almost everyone would be better off under a private system. The stock market has lumbered steadily upward ever since it started. The overall trend is always up. Historically it has outperformed every other investment vehicle. And if a person wanted a safer investment they could invest more conservatively. These are the people who might only reach the same economic level as under the current system. I suspect any few who 'under perform' under a private system will still be at least as well off, if not slightly better, than under the government system. It seems like it would be smarter for almost everyone to be better off and set up a safety net for those few who fail.

My employer and I paid a total of $155,000 into the social security system over 40 years. I will get $17,000/year at 62. If I had kept the money in a sock I would have $155,000 which could easily generate $11,000/year. I know, without rocket science investing, I could have turned that $155,000 into at least $400,000 which would easily generate $28,000/year; $11,000 more than I will have under the existing system.

We would have to require the employer and employee to continue to contribute, same as now, but they would contribute to their own plan not a government plan. It could be linked to their 401K's which have very safe investments in them. Employers already provide investment training for their 401K participants. Make this training mandatory.

By saying no to private social security the government is lowering the bar, saying citizens are not intelligent enough to invest wisely. As with anything, the less you expect the less you get. Most people could do a decent job. Most mutual fund companies have 401K funds which are tailored for those who want safety and do not want to think too much about their investments. Investing in these very conservative vehicles would guarantee your outperforming the current system with no risk of losing your investment.

Most private companies have realized providing company funded retirement is an inefficient benefit and their employees could do a better job by themselves. They have provided investment tools, often with 3-4% matching company funds, for the employee to generate their own retirement nest egg. I wish this had been available when I started work. My retirement nest egg would have been much larger with even very conservative investments. The same argument applies to social security.

Abortion is one huge cop out on responsibility. Preventing unwanted pregnancies is a good idea practiced by forward thinking, caring and intelligent people. It allows thoughtful people to plan for the number of children they can care for adequately. Where babies come from is not a mystery. Methods of prevention are abundantly known. Abortion is not pregnancy prevention. Abortion is not birth control. It is life termination and it encourages irresponsibility. We talk about learning from our mistakes but abortion encourages us to make the same mistake over and over because there is a way out. I wonder how many people could kill their baby if they had to do it themselves and watch the baby die. It is very strange, we can kill something which a few months later would be so precious to us!

Why is it a person can abort their baby and we say they are being responsible controlling their reproductive rights? And yet if the same person takes drugs or engages in other activities which endanger the health of their unborn child, we say they are irresponsible, even criminal. Why is it a person is said to be exercising their reproductive rights when they have their babies head crushed and the dead body removed from their womb and discarded? But if that same person delivered the baby and smothered it as soon as it was born and discarded it, we call them a monster.

Our country was made great because of the monetary reward provided to smart, hardworking people who come up with products benefiting mankind. I have no problem with these people making a lot of money from their effort. The alternative is to become stagnant like Russia and China were before they allowed free enterprise. It would be nice if we were all altruistic but we are not. I will gladly put up with a few stinking rich people who produce a higher standard of living for the rest of us. At least they provide something useful unlike stinking rich overpaid athletes and entertainers who do absolutely nothing except provide bad role models.

And another thing, we have way too many laws and rules. There are laws and rules for everything. And many of the laws are often not (because enforcement is virtually impossible for some laws) enforced. I will make no attempt to list all the laws on the books which are ignored but you all know there are tons of them. A law which is not enforced is worse than no law at all because people begin to ignore all laws, even the ones which are important. I mean, think about it, one of the first rules of parenting is to enforce your rules or don't have them. Take the speed limits. Virtually everyone goes in excess of 10 mph over the limit. Allowing for some error in speedometers and radar guns, people should be ticketed for 6 mph over the limit. Constantly ignoring rules creates a dangerous attitude in us. Like the frog in the pot of cold water on the stove over a flame. We keep doing more and more small things wrong (speed, cheat on income tax, foul language). Our life can become more wrong than right and we may be lulled into increasing the severity of our wrongs, eventually trashing our life.

Why do we persist in creating laws which inconvenience millions to placate a few complainers and whiners? One small example is the privacy laws which prevent a parent from obtaining needed information on college or medical insurance bills for their dependent teenagers. Teenagers who are totally dependent on their parent and have no desire to hide anything from them. The teenager pays none of these bills and has no desire to have anything to do with them and yet the parent is prevented from accessing this data unless they get the proper forms signed and filed. It would make a lot more sense if the law made those few teens (who did not want their parents to have access) fill out the forms. Rather than the current system which requires millions of tons of needless paper work.

What if we assumed everyone was honest instead of dishonest? That is how the laws seem to be set up. Think of all the time saved by not having everyone getting useless notarized signatures, etc. What does all this save? Seems to me most dishonest people are not caught by these things but all the honest people are inconvenienced.

I hear complaints, families are failing, parents are not doing their jobs. Indeed this is happening. However passing laws which negate parental authority does not help. Like no parental notification needed for a young person's abortion or birth control tools.

We would all like to avoid tragedy in our lives, but it seems we think we can legislate tragedy out of our lives. If something bad happens we pass a law with the intent of preventing future occurrences. No matter this only happened to one person in the entire world and maybe it may have been prevented by common sense. We pass a law or make a rule. Before we pass a law we need to ask "Will this law accomplish its goal? Is it enforceable? Will people do it? Can we afford it? Is this law or rule just a feel good thing (We did something)? We cannot legislate our world into safety. We cannot make everything illegal that has the remotest chance of hurting someone. No swimming allowed on this beach because there is no lifeguard. No sledding on this hill. Why not no driving? It is the most dangerous activity most of us engage in during our life. People need to be responsible for their own actions. If they wish to swim where there is no lifeguard, they need to be vigilant themselves, post their own lifeguard.

Most laws exist only because of a small minority of people who violate them. We must be careful of feel good laws and rules (We did something!) which inconvenience the majority but do little or nothing to stop the offenders. A simple example might be metal detectors in schools. A tremendous inconvenience and cost, but anyone who really wishes to can get whatever they want into the school.

Proliferation of laws and rules seems to be an effort to remove any necessity of people working things out amongst themselves, of exercising any judgment and thinking. People will make mistakes. But I would rather see someone making the best decision they can rather than blindly following some set of rigid rules. People are afraid to make any decisions for fear of being sued.

On the other hand we should make every effort to obey the laws, working to change those with which we are not in agreement. Everything we do in the world eventually comes back to us. If you cheat on your income taxes, the money must be made up in higher taxes. Keeping the money when we are given too much money at check out must result in higher prices to account for such errors. Being unkind to others results in unkindness from them and less people wanting to help us in our times of need. We think when we do these things it is not personal. Our impersonal world breeds these feelings. Everyone cheats, steals, lies, violates the laws and is unkind. This becomes the prevailing attitude. Each and everyone of us shapes the world.

Giving

We seem to have forgotten the true beauty of a gift. Today a gift is some material item bought for designated times or events. It is expected, almost required. These are not gifts, they are a duty.

A true gift is one we give for no particular reason. A gift is a symbol of one person caring for another. The gift itself is of little consequence compared to the love expressed by the giver. A gift should be spontaneous, appropriate for the moment, just the right one.... If we gave such gifts we would be giving gifts more often, but spending less. We would more often give the greatest gift we have to offer and find so difficult to give; ourselves. Our love, a helping hand, an opened door, a kind word, a smile. None of these cost a dime. What present is almost sure to bring tears to you eyes? I'll bet it is the item hand made by your child at school. Why do we let this manner of giving die to be replaced by commercialism? Material gifts are man's invention to circumvent our poor ability to properly express our love.

Ultimately gifts are earned. No one should be given gifts indefinitely if they never show their kindness in return.

Material Wants

Our reliance on material things for our happiness is causing a great deal of unhappiness. Material things are like drugs. They are exciting at first but the novelty wears off quickly and we need more, bigger, and "better" things to keep us satisfied. In a year or so you grow tired of the new car, but do you ever tire of your child's smile, a bird singing, a walk in the sunshine? All these are free!

Never envy others. There will always be someone who has more than you. Some deservedly and some not. What others have is beyond your power to control. If you want something, do your best to attain it and resolve to be happy with the results.

We make a huge production of everything these days. Are our children better off performing in a $10 million auditorium or on the tiny raised stage we had in our gym/lunchroom/auditorium? I do not think I received an inferior education. In fact it was better because I had a more humble outlook on life and fewer, "Wants". Also both my parents did not have to work to afford the taxes to pay for all this extravagance. My mother was home with us!

If the economy had to depend on me it would be in the tank. My idea of a good car is the cheapest one that will reliably get me from point A to point B. I buy clothes when I need them and wear them till they fall apart. Since fashions come and go, what was out yesterday is in today, I might be in fashion today or out. Big deal. I am on the trailing edge of technology. Because that new gadget costs 10X today what it will 1 year from now. And the advance it has over what I have is not worth 10X the money.

Real joy comes from the heart, spirit and mind. It comes from within not without. We make ourselves happy or unhappy. No one else has the power to make you unhappy unless you allow it. Learn to like yourself and the simple joys in life and you will be happy.

Lying on the warm earth
Playing games with the clouds
Watching squirrels chasing each other
Listening to the whispering trees
Inhaling the breath of the skies
Thinking this is man
Knowing joy

Nature and Conservation

Many of us never understand the power of compounding. Conservation is like managing your finances. The saying "A penny saved is a penny earned" should be the bedrock of both. Saving the individual penny is not the issue; rather it is developing a responsible attitude (There is that word attitude again). In all aspects of our life small things add up over time. "It only cost $2 per month." "I left the water running so I would not have to keep turning it on and off to rinse the dishes but I only wasted a few gallons of water." If everyone in our country has the same routine for rinsing the dishes (which many do), hundreds of millions of gallons of water are wasted every day!

Why do we stand there with the door open in winter talking to someone? Would it make more sense for the person who is out to come in or the person who is in to go out? You are wasting not only the earth's energy, but your money. The problem is people do not see the cumulative effect on both your heating bill and on the world's energy reserves. As a result of the open door your bill will probably be a few dollars higher every month. That might save you $1000 in your lifetime and there are many similar small savings possible, adding up to many thousands in your lifetime. Looking from a global perspective the waste becomes much more awesome. Hundreds of millions of dollars are wasted in the US every month of every year from simply not closing doors. But again these are only two simple examples of how we can make a difference in our life and in the world. The point is we need to change our attitude. And, as is so often true, if everyone changed their attitude the world would be a much different place.

Comfort Zones

So many people are never happy. The food, the weather, or what someone said is never quite right. Coca Cola will not do, it has to be Pepsi Cola. We must go to restaurant A. I will not go to restaurant B. People are hard to please. Life would be so much easier for them if they were less rigid on what satisfies them. In reality, in most cases, there is not that much difference between A and B and the differences are not really important anyway. Diversify your life a little. Compromise. Most things are not that important. The people you do things with are what make them fun. So almost anything is fun if you do not approach the activity with a negative attitude and enjoy the people you are with. All around me I see people seemingly at war with everyone and everything around them; quick to offend and frustrate. For most of us the world will soon forget we ever existed once we are gone. We should at least enjoy our time spent here and have some positive impact on our world. Lighten up! Enjoy life! Stop being so grouchy!

All winter long people complain about the cold, clouds and being cooped up in the house. When summer comes they keep their car windows rolled up so they won't muss their hair. They are still cooped up in the house with the windows up and the air on so they won't be hot. They even put on sunglasses so it looks like a cloudy day. Nothing is ever quite right if you have such a narrow range of acceptable climatic conditions. Somehow I think we would all be happier if we savored the moment more often just as it is. Perhaps an increased tolerance for our climate might increase our tolerance in other areas of life. It might improve our Attitude.

Rain really is not that bad. We need it. And it is so peaceful to sit and read listening to the gentle fall of rain.

Sports

I love sports. I play a multitude of sports in a reasonably proficient manner. Some sport should be a part of everyone's life, if possible.

But the current state of sports is not great. Not that everything about it is bad, but there are too many negatives. The good is losing. Too many players are negative role models. I guess there were always a lot of jerks in the professional ranks, but they were never so highly paid and visible. They owe the fans something in exchange for those huge salaries other than their performance in their sport. They say they are just people, but if they want to command huge salaries (which the fan pays) they must be better than just normal people. The fans are amazing. They say the players should get as high a salary as they can squeeze out of the owners. But the owners can only pay those high salaries with higher ticket prices and expensive commercials which are part of the increased cost to the products we buy.

How do fans remain loyal to teams where the player's only loyalty is not to the fan but to the almighty dollar? They jump to another team to make $1 million a year more than the $11 million your team is paying them! I understand they do this for their family! I guess I can see how it must be hard to make ends meet on only $11 million per year!

Youth sport is marching down the same path as the pros; everything is so intense. Practice 3 hours every day and win at all costs. I suppose this produces better athletes but at what cost? An infinitesimal number of children will make money from the sport they are playing. The value from the activity should be physical exercise, sportsmanship (what appears to me to be a dying attribute), cooperation, the simple act of participating, doing their best, enjoying it with their friends and knowing a sport they can enjoy the rest of their lives.

Parents of youths involved in sports are also often terrible role models; parents being abusive to young referees trying their best to do a good job; shouting derogatory remarks to players, coaches and parents on the other team. Abusive parents should be barred from games, for the season or longer.

Why is it in America we must have a winner? If two teams play to a tie in regulation time, why can't it be a tie? That day both teams were equal. Does tacking on a few extra minutes really prove who was better? You only need a winner when only one team can advance in a playoff situation.

Watching sports on TV is the male version of soap operas. They would be much better off playing more and watching less.

We should eliminate national teams in the Olympics. If one country wins more medals, what does this mean? Is that country an asset to the world? It is just a sporting event! It has nothing to do with self or national worth. We should make the Olympics individuals competing one against the other. In its present state it is becoming as corrupt as professional sports. The biggest countries which spend the most money win.

Why do so many people violate every rule in their sport in order to increase their possibility of winning? I thought the idea was to win the contest by being a better player not a better cheater than your opponent. I am playing to play. Whether I win or lose will not make my self worth any more of less. Rules define the sport and reduce the risk of injury. When the game is more organized there are officials to interpret and enforce the rules. But like all other life's rules, we should follow the rules in sports because it is the right thing to do not because some official is watching and might penalize us for a violation. We certainly should not purposely violate the rules to gain an unfair advantage. What happened to that good sport idea, "I could not feel I had beaten someone if I did it by pulling their jersey, tripping them, distracting them with trash talk, pushing them...."? If you do these things, your goal is no longer playing the sport as best you know how, but rather it is beating someone. This is not the spirit of sports! In fairness to current athletes, this is not a new problem but it is getting worse.

Mr. Spock

We would all be better off, if we had a little more of Mr. Spock in us. Emotion is wonderful, but so often we let it tear us apart. Emotion is great, but riding an emotional roller coaster is not. We let ourselves get way too high and way too low. Few things are overwhelmingly bad or good. Emotion should enrich our life, but it should not rule it. Rational well thought out decisions are the best direction for our life. We think love is emotion. To some extent it is, but more importantly it is a rational caring for another person. Love is (should be) earned by a person conducting their life in a manner which makes you feel good about them (love them).

Why is it we say people who want to be neat and organized are anal? Don't you like to, not miss appointments and know where your belongings are without a half hour search?

Life's Balances

All life is in a balance, some hardship with some joy, something beautiful with something less than beautiful. Rain produces rainbows and grows crops for us to eat, but we become stuck in the mud and terrible floods can result. Ever hear someone say my life was ruined by Vietnam or the death of my child, etc.? All of us have some tragedy in our life. How we cope with it determines its effect on us. The tragedy is not so much the problem as how we react. Again there is the importance of our attitude.

Differences

We are all different. Differences can make our world better or worse. We all perform some needed function. Some add knowledge, others economic prosperity, happiness, some are simply good people or perhaps raise good children. We have all heard stories about the engine that will not function for lack of one bolt. Maybe you are that bolt.

It is good to feel pride in our ethnic, religious, family background or in our athletic and scholastic accomplishments. It is bad when these differences lead us to feel and act superior or inferior. There will never be peace in our world as long as we allow differences between us to spawn hatred.

A significant step could be made toward worldwide unity by requiring everyone to learn one common language in addition to their native language. Instruction would start in kindergarten. Esperanto was a language conceived as a worldwide language in 1887. It could not have succeeded regardless of any other difficulties because the world was not ready. Admittedly it will still be very difficult to obtain worldwide agreement. However our leaders should be encouraged toward this goal because the potential resultant good is so immense. It is inevitable. It is eventually necessary if we desire to unite the world as one human race, not as fighting factions. There are many possible choices; put all languages in a hat and pick one, invent a new language or make it English (which is close to worldwide already) and have all those already speaking English learn one other language.

In the past an offshoot of our differences and the resulting conflict was technological advance which greatly advanced our species. It was probably worth the price we paid in the horrible conflicts! However I believe the time for advancing our species in that manner has ended. It is time to consider ourselves all a part of one human race first and dwell less on our ethnic and religious differences. I believe as a species we have gradually become more homogeneous and this process is accelerating. It is only a matter of time before all ethnic differences disappear, a thousand years perhaps, but eventually. Some say this is bad because diversity makes the world go round. However people will still be different in other ways. I believe decreased ethnic diversity will gradually produce a more peaceful world which will be a more powerful stimulant toward advancing our species than ethnic diversity. It is OK to be proud of your heritage, but you should be even more proud of being a human being. I suppose we could stagnate but I believe before that happens we will meet races from other star systems which will again introduce diversity and spur us ever forward. Hopefully peacefully, due to a more enlightened interaction between races.

Goals

The phrase "You can do anything if you put your mind to it" has resulted in a lot of very disappointed people. The importance of hard work and what it can overcome cannot be overemphasized. Someone who works hard at something will usually do better than a lazy person with a lot of raw talent. When someone sets a goal he must acknowledge the fact that nothing worthwhile comes without a great deal of hard work.

However realism must enter in the setting of all goals. Each of us has different abilities and disabilities that make it easier, more difficult, or impossible to attain certain goals. When a goal is set we must work as hard as we can to reach that goal and have the strength of spirit to be happy not reaching that goal if our best efforts fall short. I think this means it is important to make the most of our talents by working hard, have a realistic idea of ourselves and be happy with that.

Authority

Whatever happened to just telling people what to do? Democracy works up to a point. We elect people we think will make good decisions. They should make decisions, seems as if no one wants to make decisions. The dollar coin is a perfect example. Twice the government recently produced dollar coins; the Susan B Anthony and the Sacagawea. Both times they declared the effort a failure. People kept using the paper dollar. If we really wanted the dollar coin to succeed, the obvious solution was to stop making the paper dollar. I cannot believe our government could be that naive. It was desirable. It would have saved the tax payer's money. With the paper dollar officially out of production manufacturers of various vending machines would have realized they had to plan to modify their machines and would have had time to do this since the paper dollar would gradually fade away as they wore out. If your child was ill and needed to take some medication would you make it their option to take it? I don't think so.

Rules are an insurance policy. Rules were put there because violating them can result in harm to you or someone else. You can ignore all the rules and get away with it for awhile but eventually it catches up to you. The more rules you follow the smaller the chance you will ruin your life.

People are weird about police. They are tooling along at 78 in a 65 zone. They see the police and slow to 60!

I thought a yellow light meant, "Think about stopping", not "Step on the gas pedal" and go through a red light.

You have seen the signs, "Fines doubled for speeding in a work zone". Have you ever seen anyone stopped in a work zone? I have not. In fact, seems like what I see is: Going slightly over the 65 limit I am slowly passing a few people (I say slowly and a few because the average speed in a 65 zone must be around 75-80) when along comes a work zone with a 55 limit. Now with me going slightly over the lower limit everyone is zooming by.

Am I missing something? Do these people have only one speed? Are they in La La land? For, sure enough, if the work zone is short and you drive awhile you will soon slowly pass the same people you passed before the work zone. Of course you will never catch the others!

Our leadership is going to pot. It is sad; the only way our state and local governments can figure out to make money is to promote gambling; lotteries, horse racing and casinos. Gambling is not productive. It does nothing to produce a better future for mankind. In fact in the past it was always considered undesirable. In fact it is illegal unless sanctioned by the government so they can get a portion of the take. I mean, if we are worried about a few people losing their retirement through poor fund choices in privatized social security why don't we worry about those needlessly ruined through gambling? Is it just me or is there something not right about all this?

Exercise

We are killing ourselves with labor saving devices. We go to great lengths and expense to avoid a little physical work. But physical work is key to producing a healthier body which will allow life to be more enjoyable and longer. If you are able (and the funny thing is, if you do more physical things they will become easier) push the lawnmower instead of using one with power drive or worse yet a rider, walk instead of ride a golf cart, walk up the stairs instead of riding the escalator, walk an extra 50ft in the mall parking lot instead of wasting time and gas waiting for a spot or driving around looking for a closer spot. Does it make sense to bitterly contest a parking spot when there is another spot 10 spaces away?

People complain about having no time. Yet they ride a power mower and then go to the gym to run around a track when they could have accomplished both by pushing the mower around the yard. Can't we at least walk on the moving walkway at the airport? You would get to the end faster. People say we need these things because so many people cannot walk the distance needed. But I think more people would be able to do the walk if they exercised more.

I often hear people accuse fit people of being vain. There is a difference between vanity and wanting to keep yourself looking as good as you can. I think that is exercising personal responsibility. Even if the person is vain, they are doing something you should be doing. Staying fit even if for the wrong reason.

So many shopping carts never get put where they belong. Is it because we are lazy or just, do not think? Laziness is the worst possible reason. We are killing ourselves being lazy. Walking the cart to the collection site would not be a big deal to any of us and would provide a little exercise. Think of all the negatives. We miss a chance to exercise. Someone is inconvenienced by the shopping cart in the parking spot. The store must pay someone to round up all those carts which ultimately adds cost to your groceries.

Behavior

There has always been considerable crudeness in the world but it seems to be increasing because we promote it. In the past, we did not show it in mass media, movies, and TV. But now it is rampant. No one can convince me children are not influenced to talk and act crudely when this is what they see and hear in all the mass media. In the past, many of our children's athletic and entertainment idols were not the most couth people, but at least we required they act civilized during competition and in public. And their bad behavior was not so widely publicized. Now we put up with just about anything they do as long as they keep the money flowing.

All the incredibly crude movies and TV shows make a lot of money and have large audiences! Do these audiences want a world like this? Don't the actors and actresses feel any shame from producing such trash?

We say we want people to be honest, obey the rules, and care about others. Our idols are often the opposite. They are the high flying, flamboyant, rule breaking, constantly in trouble people. We seem to think these are the people really enjoying life. Most of these people lay a path of destruction in their lives and the lives of those close to them; drugs, broken marriages and jail litter their lives. Often the happiest people are invisible, quietly and simply enjoying life. It is just like our desire for material things, all glitz. Glitz often brings sadness, almost never happiness. Deep down we all seem to know this, but hate to admit happiness can be so simple.

I have heard we should not judge others. I think this is part of our political correctness problem today. I think if you have a strong conviction, you have a responsibility to express it. To not do so is a cop out.

Men are getting so close in touch with their female side, they have lost touch with their masculinity! Men and women were made to be different. Do women really want men to be exactly like them?

There is something I do not understand as a male. Women say they hate it when the first thing a man looks at when they meet them is their breasts. Why then do they wear clothes that say, "Look at my breasts"?

I see people express their uniqueness through their hair length or color, body piercing, clothes, car, etc.; all things which are unimportant. Wouldn't we be better off differentiating ourselves from the crowd by our behavior; working hard, caring for others, obeying the law, being a decent person....?

Epilogue

Why did I write this book?

Each of us has our own set of values and beliefs. Each of us hopes by communicating these ideas to others to influence them to see the world as we do. Obviously people write books to achieve this goal as I have written this book. The beauty of our world is, each of us can use all this information to produce our own set of beliefs and together we can keep the world moving steadily ahead to a better future based on the accumulated knowledge of previous generations.

As I grew older and raised two children, I realized how much turmoil and confusion existed in people's lives. I began to record ideas to help my children deal with all they would face. I realized what seemed simple to me was not so for many others. I felt obliged to share my insights with others. So I wrote this book.

There are only a very few basic principles that guarantee a happy life.

You must like yourself. Without yourself you have nothing.

You must care about everyone else in the world.

You must have a positive attitude

You must always be thinking.

Happiness is within everyone's grasp. I hope some will come closer to attaining happiness through reading this book.

One last thought. People want to be happy. They long for peace in their life. They revere various religious figures and wish the world emulated more of their values. Yet these same people make fun of and call boring people attempting to do just that!

www.ingramcontent.com/pod-product-compliance
Lightning Source LLC
Chambersburg PA
CBHW020252290526
45784CB00003B/1215